© Crown copyright 1977
First published 1957
Second Edition 1977

HER MAJESTY'S STATIONERY OFFICE

Government Bookshops

49 High Holborn, London WC1V 6HB
13a Castle Street, Edinburgh EH2 3AR
41 The Hayes, Cardiff CF1 1JW
Brazennose Street, Manchester M60 8AS
Southey House, Wine Street, Bristol BS1 2BQ
258 Broad Street, Birmingham B1 2HE
80 Chichester Street, Belfast BT1 4JY

*Government publications are also available
through booksellers*

The full range of Museum publications
is displayed and sold at the
National Maritime Museum, Greenwich

Obtainable in the United States of America
from Pendragon House Inc.
2595 East Bayshore Road
Palo Alto
California 94303

Printed in England for Her Majesty's Stationery Office
by Ebenezer Baylis and Son Limited, The Trinity Press, Worcester, and London.
Dd 290420 K 10/77

ISBN 0 11 881400 1

Cover illustrations

(Front cover) **Uniform for Special Men 1777.** Dominic Serres, merchant shipmaster turned painter, draws a sailor with interesting headgear. This is one of the crew of an Admiral's barge and he wears a hard cap not unlike a jockey's, which carries a badge on the upturned false peak. (See Plate 15.) Caps of this sort were worn by Thames watermen and are still seen in the dress of the Queen's Bargemaster and the royal watermen. Admiral Lord Anson is said to have dressed his barge's crew as Thames watermen and a lead from such a famous figure could well have set a trend.
Etching by D Serres. Department of Pictures, National Maritime Museum.

Frontispiece **The Old and the New 1975.** In 1975 modifications which make for more comfort, ease of maintenance and a general streamlining of seamen's dress, were approved and will be introduced. The bell-bottomed trousers, creased horizontally as a result of having been lashed up in a bundle to stow in a kit-bag, will give way to flared trousers with a fore-edge crease. The black *silk* will become a facing to the jumper, needing no ribbons to tie it down. The lanyard, long since bereft of its clasp kife, now disappears.
MOD (Navy) Photograph.

(inside back cover) **Fore and Aft Rig 1977.** Fleet Chief Petty Officer, and *(left)* a Petty Officer. The wearing of a double-breasted 'long' jacket as distinct from the shorter 'round' jacket and straight cut trousers for Chief Petty Officers dates from 1899.
National Maritime Museum photograph.

(back cover) **The WRNS, a Jubilee Study 1917 and 1977.** Dictates of fashion alter the height of the hemline from time to time but the Wren ratings of the Second World War wore the 'fore and aft' rig of jacket and skirt with blue badges, although several different working rigs existed. The Leading Wren (right) wears the shoulder flash of the Women's Royal Naval Reserve and the cap tally HMS *President*, headquarters ship of the London Division. At the left, a Wren uniform of 1917–19 from the Museum's Collection.
National Maritime Museum photograph.

ƆLLEGE

The Dress of the British Sailor

Compiled by
Admiral Sir Gerald Dickens KCVO, CB, CMG
(1879–1962)

Published for the Trustees of the National Maritime Museum by
Her Majesty's Stationery Office, London

Foreword

Twenty years have gone by since this little book first appeared, on the centenary of the introduction of uniform for petty officers and men of the Royal Navy. In bringing out a new edition we have felt it unseemly to tamper with the writings of a grandson of Charles Dickens, although we have changed a large number of the pictures.

The value of original contemporary illustrations, even if they are only caricatures, is felt to be greater than that of most reconstructions. Now, therefore, all the pictures of sailors which we have chosen show them as seen by their fellow men, artists as well as photographers. Where further comment has been needed, it has been put into the captions.

In this second edition we are happy to welcome the ladies in pictures showing uniforms of ratings of the Women's Royal Naval Service, in this their Diamond Jubilee year.

The working dress of seamen evolved because of the nature of their daily tasks. The wet, the cold, the pitch and tar, the wear and chafe, the clambering aloft and the paddling about on deck, all these demanded clothes appropriate to the sea life and which, incidentally, you could tell a mile off.

The bulk supply of 'slops', originally meaning essential garments to clothe the lower regions, and later applied to all a seaman's clothes, led to a measure of uniformity. By the early years of Victoria's reign naval ratings were wearing wide-legged trousers, jumpers or blouses, straw hats and knotted handkerchiefs, a dress which was adopted and regulated by Admiralty Order 120 years ago. The miniature sailor suit worn by the Prince of Wales, later King Edward VII, I would particularly commend to your notice. It is an important survival showing the authentic garments a decade before the 1857 Regulations.

Little by little the dress of the British sailor has been modified and the process is still going on, but the seaman of a nuclear submarine in his shore-going rig is still a recognizable descendant of his Nelsonian forebear.

John Munday MA FSA
Keeper Department of Weapons & Antiquities
National Maritime Museum

Introduction

Early Times

We have to go back to the Roman occupation of Britain for the earliest reference to the dress of the British seaman, and we find that the men who manned the fast sailing craft, maintained to give intelligence of hostile vessels, wore blue. After many centuries and changes of colour, the British sailor's uniform again became, and has remained, blue.

Before we say anything more about dress or uniform, we must ask you to remember that there was no general official uniform until the middle of the nineteenth century. Moreover, prior to the reign of Charles II naval forces were made up of a few royal ships reinforced by armed merchant vessels, the Cinque Ports being required to furnish the greater number of these. For all that, we do see that at any particular period there was a certain similarity in the costume of seamen, and this was only natural for, like all other bodies, a fashion evolved which was largely dictated by the nature and the peculiarities of ship life.

Attempts were periodically made to establish some sort of uniform, but these were generally of a local nature. For instance, we read that in the reign of Henry I special clothing was provided for the Cinque Port sailors: '*A tunic of rough coarse woollen cloth dyed blue, drawers, stockings and shoes.*' Again, when in 1553 Sir Hugh Willoughby's expedition to discover the North-East Passage left the Thames the mariners were all '*apparelled in Watchet or skie-coloured cloth*'.

There was another complication in those early days, which made for a great diversity of costume in a ship's company, namely, that half the latter were composed of mariners and the rest of men-at-arms and crossbowmen (that is to say, 'soldiers') embarked to do the fighting, the mariners confining themselves on the whole to working the ships. Here again there must have been some confusion in apparel as, although the 'soldiers' wore armour, it was not uncommon for the seaman to do the same.

'Jackettes' for seamen are mentioned in the reign of Edward IV. They were short body garments, belted, cut low in the neck, with wide sleeves to the elbow. We hear also of green and white tunics

with a cross of St George as a badge. Later, a petticoat is mentioned, which was, in fact, a small coat protruding beneath the doublet.

The Stuart Period

A factor making for a semblance of uniformity in dress was the 'slop' system whereby certain articles of clothing and materials, made to specifications laid down by the Navy Commissioners, were sold on board ships to the seamen under the supervision of the purser. It was, however, optional for the seamen to buy them. We first hear of this system in 1623. The articles sold seem to have been confined to canvas jackets, waistcoats and underclothing. There were, however, many abuses among pursers and slop-sellers, with the consequence that supplies were often inadequate both in quantity or quality. It frequently happened that some ships failed to get any supplies at all. Added to this, ships' companies were paid so irregularly and at such long intervals (one of the main grievances leading to the Mutiny at Spithead, 1797) that, in the early days, the men were often not in a position to purchase what they needed. This drawback was, however, rectified by an ordinance to the effect that after a man had been two months in a ship he could get slops on credit to an amount not exceeding ten shillings every two months. This arrangement could not have been popular with the slop sellers, seeing that they had to wait until the ship paid off before they could get their money.

Matters improved in the reign of Charles II who took a personal interest in the outfitting of his sailors; the variety of slops was extended and the Treasury assisted payments by means of grants. Here is an extract from certain instructions issued by the Duke of York in 1663: '*Cloaths worn by seamen – Monmouth caps, red caps, yarn stockings, Irish stockings, blue shirts, white shirts, cotton waistcoats, blue neckcloths, canvas suits and rugs, which are alone permitted to be sold.*'

The forerunner of the sailor's collar makes its appearance at about this time – a collar of cambric or linen falling on the shoulders.

Previous to the Dutch Wars (1653–1673), the King's ships being few in number and only reinforced by mercantile vessels as occasion demanded, our sea forces were usually small and scattered. The

Plate 1 English Seaman 1598. Northern sailors are characterized by voluminous trousers and furry caps. The Venetian Vecelli records this Englishman in his book of *Costume Old and New*. *Woodcut. Courtesy British Museum.*

Dutch wars, however, fought mainly in the Channel and North Sea, produced massive and concentrated fleets. This, naturally enough, tended to a greater uniformity in the clothing of sailors, as indeed it did in other naval matters. The subsequent wars against the French show an increase in this tendency.

We read that our seamen who fought at the battles of Beachy Head (1690) and La Hogue (1692) wore blue waistcoats, Kersey jackets, white petticoat-breeches with red cross stripes, red caps and white neckcloths.

Eighteenth Century

The beginning of the eighteenth century forms a very definite epoch in naval dress. The slop organisation had grown and, judging by Navy Board files, the authorities took great pains to see that seamen were given a good range of clothes of good material at fair prices from which to select.

Here are some of the items mentioned in a contract made by the Commissioners of the Admiralty with a Mr Richard Harnage in 1706: '*Shrunk grey Kersey jacket, lined with red cotton with 15 brass buttons and two Poketts of Linnen, the Button-holes sticht with Gold coloured Thread, at Ten Shillings and Six Pence. Waistcoat of Welsh Red plain unlined with Eighteen Brass Buttons, the holes sticht with gold coloured Thread at five Shillings and sixpence. Red Kersey Breeches . . . Three Leather Pocketts and Thirteen White tin Buttons – Five Shillings and sixpence.*'

There were also mentioned: '*Red flowered Shag breeches (5/6d); Strip'd Breeches, Blew and White Chequr'd Linnen Shirts (3/3d). Ditto Drawers (2/3d); Leather Cap faced with Red Cotton (1/2d), Grey Woolen Stockings (1/9d), Double Sold Shoes.*'

In 1762 the *London Chronicle* tells us that 'sailors wore the sides of their hats uniformly tacked down to the crown, and looked as if they carried a triangular apple pasty upon their heads'.

The above patterns altered considerably towards the end of the eighteenth century. Blue began to predominate; the jacket, which formerly had been grey, was now blue, so were breeches and waistcoats. The jackets were double-breasted with eight buttons ('mettle') with an anchor. Black silk handkerchiefs round the neck were often worn. The cocked hat for the seamen became a thing of the past.

Plate 2   Early Georgian Sailor 1737. The celebrated statue known as the Farnese Hercules stands clothed as a British sailor. His trousers are loose-fitting, his knotted kerchief and little three-cornered hat jauntily worn, are all essential ingredients of the sea costume.

His 'I wait for Orders' is evidently intended to ridicule the pacific policies of Walpole, in the face of allegations of cruelties and depradations by the Spaniards; war was to break out in 1739.

Etching. Courtesy British Museum.

Plate 3 Two Seamen. On the left in blue jacket and trousers is a figure which could well be the back view of the man in Plate 16. His shipmate wears a different but equally distinctive rig with the sailor's protective canvas overskirt and a fur or wool 'Monmouth' cap.
Etching by J A Atkinson, 1808. Department of Pictures, National Maritime Museum.

Early Nineteenth Century

There was still no uniform for the men of the Navy, but it may be said that a 'customary dress' came more and more into favour, e.g. white trousers, blue jacket, tarpaulin hat (straw hats coming more into fashion). Pig-tails were worn on the lower deck some time after officers had ceased to wear them. Petticoats continued into the 1820s. However, although the above articles could be drawn from the purser's stores little or no attempt was made, at least in some ships, to encourage uniformity, in fact, in many ships 'any decent clothes', *faute de mieux*, would pass muster with their captains. On the other hand, some captains introduced uniforms of their own design and at their own expense to be worn by at least part of their ship's company, especially by the crew of the captain's gig; the result being expensive and also eccentric. Here is an item from *The Times* in October, 1805: '*The Tribune, frigate, now attached to the Squadron under Sir Sydney Smith, is no less remarkable for the gallantry than the coxcombry of her crew. . . . Every man wears a smart round Japan hat with green inside the leaf, a broad gold lace band, with the name of the ship painted in front in capital letters; black silk neckerchief, with a white flannel waistcoat bound with blue; and over it a blue jacket, with three rows of gold buttons very close together, and blue trousers.*' Even as late as 1820 the Captain of the *Harlequin* dressed his gig's crew as harlequins.

But whatever the clothing or uniform made available, the sailors invariably made decorative additions to their new clothes – piping of silk or canvas in the seams of their jackets, braid trimmings, rows of bright buttons and gaudy hat ribbons with or without a name or motto on them, and so forth. Such embellishments were much in favour at the time of Trafalgar, and indeed, for the best part of a century afterwards.

Latter Half of the Nineteenth Century

In 1857 the seaman's uniform was at last definitely established. It was based on the general pattern of the dress most in use at the time. It remains the basis of the uniform in the Navy of today.

The uniform consisted of: a blue serge frock, a jumper being added as an alternative at a later date (note that the jumper overlaps the trousers, the frock is tucked into them); blue collar bordered

Plate 4   Sailor 1849. The blue jean collar, ornamented with a row or rows of white tape, is worn outside the short blue cloth jacket; the straw sennit hat with its name ribbon, as variously worn, takes on the character of its wearer. Compare this print with the photograph of some thirty years later (Plate 30). They could be men from the same ship.
Lithograph by J Harris after R H C Ubsdell. Department of Pictures, National Maritime Museum.

with white tape, blue cloth jacket, blue cloth trousers, duck or white drill frock and duck trousers as alternatives to the serge and cloth; pea jacket; black silk handkerchief; sennit hat (straw), black or white according to the climate; blue cloth cap; badges of rank for Petty Officers.

A word about the collar. A legend arose, and still persists, that the three rows of white tape were to commemorate the three great victories of Nelson – The Nile, Copenhagen and Trafalgar. No such sentimental idea stirred the breasts of the people concerned at the Admiralty for, at one time, the merits of two stripes as against three were canvassed. The black silk handkerchief is understood by many to exist as a badge of mourning for Nelson's death. It *may* be so, but we can find no proof of this, and it must be remembered that black silk handkerchiefs were often worn by sailors before the time of Trafalgar.

Boots and shoes had always figured in a sailor's outfit, but certainly in the nineteenth and early part of the twentieth centuries they were worn as little as possible on board. The consequence was that the sailors' feet were flat, and their soles as hard as any leather, and so, when they had to put on footwear they suffered great discomfort; indeed, when landed to march it was not uncommon to see some of them at the end of the day getting along on bare feet, their boots slung round their necks.

The 1857 regulations do not appear to have laid down anything hard and fast as regards the form of shirt to be worn either by petty officers or ratings for in 1880 we see the Captain of one of HM ships writing: '*At present white shirts, coloured shirts, flannel shirts, paper collars and false fronts present anything but a uniform appearance.*'

When we begin to deal with the latter part of the nineteenth century the term 'seamen', which so far we have been able to use comprehensively, now needs some modification due to the appearance of the Engine Room, and the development of the Paymaster's and Medical branches, and as time went on, the creation of other specialist branches. As regards the Engine Room branch all artificers and Chief Stokers were dressed as Chief Petty Officers, blue serge or cloth jackets, waistcoat and trousers, white shirt, collar and tie, peaked cap – known as 'fore and aft rig'. Stokers and Stoker Petty Officers were, and are, dressed as Seamen and Seamen Petty Officers. All members of the other branches mentioned wore

Plate 5 A Boy Seaman HMS Brisk 1860. The frock is a wide loose-fitting garment worn tucked into the trousers. There were no pockets, hence the white handkerchief hanging out of the waistband. Most sailors smoked a pipe (generally a clay) and the only place to stow it, and other odds and ends, was inside the cap. Note the long ends of the cap ribbon, the name is probably painted on and there are two decorative motifs but no HMS.
Historic Photograph Collection, National Maritime Museum.

8

fore and aft rig until 1956 when it was decided that those below the rating of Petty Officer should be dressed as seamen.

Despite the new and detailed regulations the sailor could not be weaned from adding such additions and alterations to his uniform as he judged would improve it. This flouting of Whitehall ordinances brought a blast from the Admiralty in 1890 in the shape of a letter to all concerned. '*It has been brought to the notice of My Lords Commissioners of the Admiralty that there has been considerable laxity in observance of the Instructions laid down in the Uniform Regulations . . .*' Fresh and more stringent regulations soon appeared, but some laxity continued into the early nineteen-hundreds. In those days many men made their own clothes on board, Thursday afternoons ('Rope Yarn Sundays' in naval parlance) being officially set aside for this purpose, the bosun's mate piping 'Hands Make and Mend Clothes' (the expression still stands whenever a Ship's Company is allowed a half-holiday from ship's work), and were thus enabled to practise some independence in design. Despite the displeasure of Their Lordships and the increasing severity of ships' officers, sartorial deviationists were still to be found; but their extravagances were now confined to the dress which they reserved for leave on shore. Then one would see the bell bottoms of the trousers twice the width allowed, flannels cut very low, the blue top edge of the latter embroidered with flowers, and other decorative touches. Another touch of dandyism was a little circular mirror let into the inside of the crown of the straw hat, the wearer thus from time to time being enabled to satisfy himself as to his appearance. There is no gainsaying the fact that the bluejacket thus arrayed was a most attractive figure.

This long-drawn-out struggle against complete uniformity is after all not to be wondered at, the sailor, although amenable to the best form of discipline to be found anywhere, being by the very nature of his calling inclined, in certain respects, to some freedom of action and improvisation.

Changes in the uniform between 1857 and today have been gradual and, individually, not drastic. The blue jacket (worn over the jumper or frock) disappeared in 1891; the frock went in 1906, except in the case of Royal Yachtsmen, who still wear them. The straw hat was abolished in 1921, and replaced in hot climates by pith helmets. The flannel (shirt) was replaced by a white cotton

Plate 6   A 1st Class PO 1897. This petty officer also appears in working rig in Plate 35. Here he has shifted into No 1 rig. His first class petty officer's crown and crossed anchors with two good conduct badges is in gold wire, while on his other sleeve are his gunnery qualifications and marksman's badge. A blue serge frock is his 'best' and the straw hat, made of coiled woven sennit, bound with blue tape, has, could we but see it, the black ribbon with the name HMS *Edinburgh* in woven gold wire. The straw hat went out of use in 1921.
Navy & Army Illustrated. National Maritime Museum Library.

vest in 1938. Not so many years ago tropical rig became white shirt and white shorts.

From the first inception of submarines their crews have worn white sweaters instead of jumpers when 'running'.

New Uniforms for the Royal Navy

We come now to the up-to-date uniforms of the Chief and Petty Officers and the men of the Royal Navy as modified in the year 1956, when new regulations of a novel character were brought into effect. Although at present much reduced in size the Navy is still vital to the safety of our country, and that being so, all of us must be interested in everything connected with it. We therefore give these regulations in some detail.

The new uniform retains the traditional 'square rig' of collar, jumper and bell-bottomed trousers, but is given added smartness by the new coat-style, zip-fronted jumper and the smoother, yet even harder wearing 'diagonal' serge cloth that has been selected. The trousers are also zip fastened and have side and hip pockets. A new type of blue jean collar combined with waistcoat is still undergoing trials. The new uniform will also be issued in white drill for appropriate occasions.

Naval personnel in all commands will wear white headgear throughout the year instead of, as previously, blue caps in the winter months in the United Kingdom; the white tops of the caps will in future be made of plastic.

All will agree as to the smartness of the new patterns, and that the uniform of the British sailor is worthy of him and as hard to beat – as he is himself.

The Naval Reserves

A most important part of our naval forces is to be found in, firstly, the Royal Naval Reserve which consists of officers and ratings drawn from the Merchant Navy and the Fisheries, and, secondly, the Royal Naval Volunteer Reserves. All of these, officers and ratings, when on naval service, wear the uniform (with certain distinctive marks) of the Royal Navy.*

* The reserves were combined as the Royal Naval Reserve in 1958.

Plate 7 The Engine Room Branch 1917. Stoker Petty Officer Pollard was serving in HM Torpedo-boats, 'small ships', which perhaps explains why he is wearing a jersey of a fancy knit with a white cap. The white shirt or *flannel* was worn in summer with the white cap, whereas a blue cap went with the seaman's blue winter jersey. His black *silk* is still the yard square but is carefully folded and his cap ribbon with a very elaborate bow is placed over the eye, not over the ear where regulations required it to be. Shoes with the toe-caps were not 'pusser', ie not of the pattern supplied by the Purser who by this time was called the Paymaster.
Historic Photograph Collection, National Maritime Museum.

The Naval Forces of the Commonwealth

It must be remembered – it is often forgotten in this country – that the navies of the Commonwealth countries are directly under the orders of their own governments. But, as in other things in our freely bound Commonwealth, the navies work in the closest possible touch, are bound by similar traditions and customs, and so it may be said that, to all intents and purposes, naval uniform in all parts of the Commonwealth is, and will always be, the same.

The Women's Royal Naval Service

In both World Wars women served with the Navy, helping to run a wide range of services on shore and some afloat, releasing men for fighting duty with the fleet.

WRNS ratings, first recruited in 1917, wore a long navy serge dress with a small blue jean sailor collar and a soft hat with cap ribbon. They had working overalls and wore badges of a light blue. The Wrens of 1939 wore a navy jacket and skirt with the soft hat replaced in 1942 by the sailor cap. There were working rigs including bell-bottoms for boats' crews.

In 1949 the Women's Royal Naval Service became a permanent part of the Royal Navy.

A Postscript

In 1975, after trials of a variety of designs including a blue-jacket, a modified version of the sailor's 'square rig' was approved and the changeover is to be gradual.

The bell-bottomed trousers with their characteristic creases will be replaced by flared trousers with a fore-edge crease.

The black *silk* will become a vestigial facing to the jumper and the blue jean collar will be attached by *velcro*.

The white lanyard, which for years has had nothing but a loop on the end, since seamen ceased to require a jack-knife on all occasions, will disappear.

Uniforms for sailors will be tailor made, not 'slop' issue and one suit will be in rough serge and the other, for best, will be in diagonal serge.

Plate 8 WRNS 1917. 'Release a man for sea service' said the recruiting posters, and the determined young women who joined up in the First World War wore the dark blue dress of the Women's Royal Naval Service, with a small version of the sailor's blue jean collar.

Plate 9 **Elizabethan Seamen 1588.** A book of charts *The Mariner's Mirror* was published in the year of the Spanish Armada, a translation from the Dutch. The figures grouped about the great circular mirror have been redrawn for the English edition. The man on the right wears a thrum cap, a long *rugge* watch-coat, full-length trousers, a doublet and has a knife on a line round his waist. The headgear of the others includes hats, caps and bonnets, and the left-hand figure wears a cloak which seems to have a hood like a duffel coat. Compare with Vecelli's sailor, Plate 1. *National Maritime Museum Library.*

(above) Plate 11 **The British Sailor's Loyal Toast 1738.** Two figures from a small rare print have been redrawn to show the petticoat-breeches or slops, 'the wide-knee'd breeches worn by seamen' according to Baileys *Dictionary* (1724), and the *mariner's cuff*, opening to allow it to be turned right back out of the wet. *National Maritime Museum.*

(left) Plate 10 **Representative Figures 1693.** Seamen of William III's time support the symbols of ship-building and navigation. The thrum cap, which could also perhaps be fur, and the kilt-like over-skirt in a check material to protect the breeches, are now recognizable as sailors' garb. The arms granted to Arthur Herbert, who was made Lord Torrington in 1689, included supporters dressed as sailors. They had wide white breeches 'double checked crosswise' in red. These figures are similarly attired. *National Maritime Museum Library.*

Plate 12 The Sailor's Farewell 1744. Ever popular in print, in pottery, in verse and in song, the sailor's leave-taking shows a typically rigged seaman. The introduction in 1747 of uniform for officers, coats of dark blue faced with white and gilt buttons with gold lace, may well have had its effect on seamen's clothes although not at once. Red and grey which had been popular colours on the quarter-deck as well as in slop clothing were seen no more among the officers and it seems likely they gradually found less favour among the men.

Engraving by C Mosley. Department of Pictures, National Maritime Museum.

Plate 13 The Sailor's Return 1744. The happy return differs from most scenes of this type, and there were many. This sailor has been round the world with Commodore Anson and after four arduous years is dressed in such finery as could only go with a big share of prize money. Indeed, wagon No 25 in the background, flying the Spanish ensign under the British, carries part of the treasure taken from the Acapulco galleon in the Pacific. Now, guarded by armed sailors and soldiers, it is on its triumphant way to London. The gold laced waistcoat might of course be loot, nor are the breeches and stockings a seaman's working dress. The gold-headed cane is not much of a substitute for a cudgel, but the sailor exhibits his characteristic *apple-pasty* hat (see p 5).

Engraving by Boitard. Department of Pictures, National Maritime Museum.

Plate 14 Combined Operations 1759. The flat-bottomed boats for landing troops are manned by sailors, and this model shows delightfully how they were dressed in the 'slop' clothing, obtained from the Purser. This was supplied by clothing contractors to Navy specifications; it was not a uniform but the garments very much of a type. The Navy Slop Office was established in 1756 to deal with this supply of contract clothing. *Department of Ships, National Maritime Museum.*

Plate 15 Bargemen's Caps c. 1780. On the right in brown velvet bearing the embroidered crest of Admiral Lord Hood. On the left in blue with white trimmings, bearing the crest of Rear Admiral Richard Edwards 1779.
Right. By courtesy of Rt Hon Viscount Hood. Left. Department of Weapons & Antiquities. National Maritime Museum.

Plate 16 Taking Soundings. His blue jacket has many small buttons and the slashed *mariner's cuff*. His straw hat (which does not seem to bear the ship's name or a ribbon), his striped shirt and the spotted neckerchief are typical.
Etching by J A Atkinson, 1808. Department of Pictures, National Maritime Museum.

Plate 18 Tom Truelove's Knell 1795. Apart from the blue jackets no two garments are the same and while Tom wears petticoat-breeches, the other is in striped trousers, both however are meant to be instantly recognizable as sailors.
Mezzotint. Published Haines & Son. Department of Pictures, National Maritime Museum.

Plate 17 A Sailor and his Lass. This pretty pair showing the ever popular theme in three dimensions, are known in various colours and are probably by Ralph Wood *c* 1775. The man's dress is similar to Plates 2 and 12.
From the Captain A C Fawssett Collection, Department of Weapons & Antiquities, National Maritime Museum.

(right) Plate 19 Seamen, 1779. A rare caricature by 'I.P.' of seamen in characteristic attitudes of caring-for-no-man, is part of a set published in London. The detail of dress, presumably authentic, is interesting; hat brims are turned up but not cocked, many-buttoned jackets have a stand-up collar with a kerchief worn outside. The slop-hose have a broad waistband and button.
Redrawn from The British Fleet. Commander C N Robinson RN, 1895. National Maritime Museum.

Plate 20 The East End of the Town 1793. A Sailor's Farewell:
waiting to embark. Seated on his sea chest he is saying good bye to his
girl and her two friends.

The reflective quality of the scene must mean a parting; they have had
their fling and now look forward to his return, who knows when, with
money to burn.

*Aquatint after Singleton. Department of Pictures, National Maritime
Museum.*

Plate 21 Dance and Skylark 1798. Stothard's pictorial idyll is staged
on the forecastle of a ship at anchor with a couple of fair charmers already
come aboard and the grog bowl in evidence. The young seaman at the
right executes the steps of a dance, with his ribboned hat and cudgel and
attired in his familiar wide-legged petticoat-breeches. A fiddler in concert
pose provides the music.

The pipe, 'Hands to Dance and Skylark', was reckoned to give the men
a chance to work some of the stiffness out of their frames after the crowded
and damp messdeck conditions.

*Mezzotint by W Ward after T Stothard. Department of Pictures, National
Maritime Museum.*

Plate 22 A Gig's Crew 1808. These seamen are dressed in a strange costume which probably denotes they are the crew of the captain's five-oared gig belonging to a man of war. This calls to mind the commander of the *Harlequin* who is said to have put his personal boat's crew into a dress representing the character from the Italian Comedy. A smart turn-out was the aim, but this print gives no clue to the name of the ship. *Etching by J A Atkinson, 1808. Department of Pictures, National Maritime Museum.*

Plate 23 The Last Jig or Adieu to Old England 1818. By comparison with the Stothard, Plate 21, this rollicking Rowlandson shows the same scene twenty years later. Female fashions have changed but the caricaturist's punch probably gets nearer the true manner of the times.

The dance, whether hornpipe, reel or jig, was as popular and widespread on board ship as on shore.

Etching by T Rowlandson. Department of Pictures, National Maritime Museum.

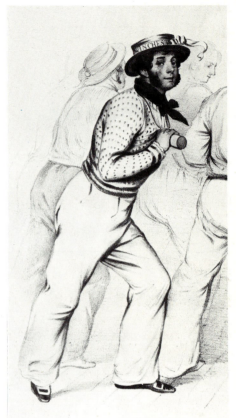

Plate 24   The Chaplain's Sketch 1812. The Rev Edward Mangin's drawing gives us a good picture of a seaman on board HMS *Gloucester* towards the end of the Napoleonic War. The tall glazed hat has not only the name of the ship on it, but also some rampant beast, perhaps the ship's badge or the Captain's crest. *Watercolour from Mangin's Journal. Department of Manuscripts, formerly in Sir Bruce Ingram's Collection, National Maritime Museum.*

Plate 25   Man-of-War's Man 1828. More like a fashion plate, this print of a sailor from a set of lithographs of naval figures, is the *blue-jacket* we are beginning to expect. His fall front trousers are of a pattern which lasted in seamen's dress until 1956. *Lithograph by M Gauci. Department of Pictures, National Maritime Museum.*

Plate 26   Weighing Anchor 1830. The 'spotted' jumper looks more like a knitted jersey and is similarly depicted in other illustrations of this time. The hat begins to look like a *boater* but was known as a round hat, as distinct from the sennit hat which got its name from the weave of the straw, a flat sennit. *Department of Pictures, National Maritime Museum.*

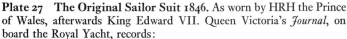

Plate 27 The Original Sailor Suit 1846. As worn by HRH the Prince of Wales, afterwards King Edward VII. Queen Victoria's *Journal*, on board the Royal Yacht, records:

'September 2, 1846 . . . Bertie put on his sailor's dress, a new one, beautifully made by the man who makes for our men. When Bertie appeared the Officers & men (who had asked permission to do so) were all assembled on deck, & cheered him, seeming quite delighted.'

Photograph courtesy of Prudence Cuming Associates Limited. Department of Weapons & Antiquities. National Maritime Museum.

Plate 28 The Russian War 1854–55. The cut of the blouse-like *frock* is of the approved pattern with low set full sleeves gathered at wrist band and with its own large square collar over which the scrubbed blue jean was worn. These sailors are all wearing their kerchiefs inside their collars. A couple of years later it was more or less this rig which became the first sailors' uniform by order of Admiralty circular No 283 of 30th January 1857.

Illustrated London News. Woodcut by W Thomas. National Maritime Museum Library.

Plate 29   The Gig's Crew of HMS Harrier 1864. Centre is the petty officer; the soft caps with long ribbons and the loose frocks tucked into the trousers. The ship's name is painted on the cap ribbons, with additional decoration. Woven wire names were adopted in 1868. The man seated at the left has a patterned kerchief inside his collar.
Photograph by courtesy of Captain J K Douglas-Morris RN.

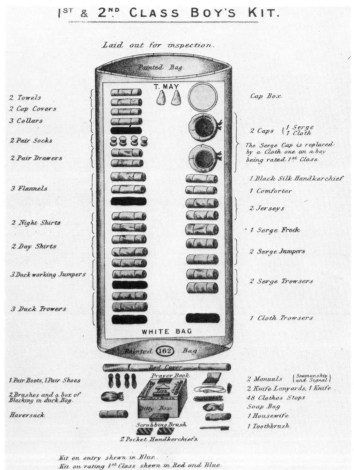

1ST & 2ND CLASS BOY'S KIT.

Laid out for inspection.

Painted Bag

T. MAY

2 Towels
2 Cap Covers
3 Collars
2 Pair Socks
2 Pair Drawers
3 Flannels
2 Night Shirts
2 Day Shirts
3 Duck working Jumpers
3 Duck Trowers

WHITE BAG

Painted (162) *Bag*

Cap Box

2 Caps { 1 Serge / 1 Cloth
The Serge Cap is replaced by a Cloth one on a boy being rated 1st Class.

1 Black Silk Handkerchief
1 Comforter
2 Jerseys
1 Serge Frock
2 Serge Jumpers
2 Serge Trowsers
1 Cloth Trowsers

Red Cover
Prayer Book

1 Pair Boots, 1 Pair Shoes
2 Brushes and a box of Blacking in duck Bag.
Haversack

Ditty Box

Scrubbing Brush
2 Pocket Handkerchiefs.

2 Manuals { Seamanship and Signal
2 Knife Lanyards, 1 Knife
48 Clothes Stops
Soap Bag
1 Housewife
1 Toothbrush

Kit on entry shewn in Blue.
Kit on rating 1st Class shewn in Red and Blue.

(above) Plate 31   Mustering Kit 1898. To live, as sailors did, with all one's clothes in a kit bag required methodical folding, tying up and stowing. Boys entering the Navy were trained in this art and had to lay out their gear and possessions in a prescribed order for inspection.
National Maritime Museum Library.

(left) Plate 30   Portrait Group 1879. The black kerchief, known accurately as a 'silk', was a yard square and could be worn, as shown here, in various ways. Today it survives but will soon merely be a facing to the jumper. The buttons on the jacket are black horn, bearing the crown and anchor. Compare with the print of 1849, Plate 4.
Historic Photograph Collection, National Maritime Museum.

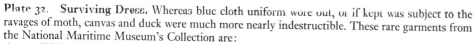

Plate 32. **Surviving Dress.** Whereas blue cloth uniform wore out, or if kept was subject to the ravages of moth, canvas and duck were much more nearly indestructible. These rare garments from the National Maritime Museum's Collection are:
(top) White frock, Petty Officer 2nd Class. Watch stripe on right shoulder. *c.* 1855 *(Bottom)* White frock, A.B., worn by J E Moore. *c.* 1855 *(Right)* White jumper, Petty Officer Wiltshire 1879 *(Left)* White frock 1867 pattern.
Department of Weapons & Antiquities, National Maritime Museum.

Plate 33 **Egyptian Campaign 1882.**
After the bombardment of Alexandria, the bearded Jack Tar is in landing rig, wearing the straight-bladed cutlass-bayonet for his Martini-Henry rifle.
Woodcut, Illustrated London News. National Maritime Museum Library.

Plate 34 Manning the Navy 1860. Full of anecdote, this painting includes a recruiting Petty Officer wearing the winter rig of tarred straw hat and blue jacket with badges. The rest of the party, on top of the coach, is making a day of it, with a variety of headgear in evidence. One is left wondering whether the young prize-winning waterman will leave home and beauty and enlist in Her Majesty's Navy.

Oil painting by G B O'Neil. Department of Pictures, National Maritime Museum. Exhibited.

Plate 35 Some Key Men, HMS Edinburgh 1897. A posed group of petty officers at Queen Victoria's Diamond Jubilee Review of the Fleet at Spithead. Left, white duck working jumper, etc. Third man: blue jumper with white lanyard. Fourth man: blue frock (tucked into trousers), no lanyard and rather battered cap, probably worn only on board. The frock was abolished in 1906. Fifth man: the same with the addition of a white lanyard, not conspicuously worn. See also Plate 6. Sixth man: same, with bare feet, quite usual on board. Seventh man: this barefoot petty officer is a Boatswain's Mate. Instead of a lanyard he wears a thin chain on the end of which is a boatswain's call. His jumper has a special pocket for it. Badges are in red wool for blue uniform and blue for white uniform. The dark blue jean collar, after repeated washing, took on a paler shade, a phenomenon familiar in the present age.
Navy & Army Illustrated. National Maritime Museum Library.

23

Plate 36 Caps, Ribbons and Badges 1879–1977. In view of the Navy's use of traditional ship names, it is sometimes difficult to decide which vessel of a particular name is represented by the ribbon.

The complexity of naval badges is shown in this selection from the Museum's collection including gold wire, red wool, blue wool and blue **printed** badges.